JOURNEY

of the

ROSE

Helen- For the
many things we both
love & have shared — beauty,
drama, students, Greece.

Enjoy!
Gloria J. Burgess

JOURNEY
of the
ROSE

Poems by
Gloria Burgess

JAZZ MEDIA
Edmonds, Washington

Publisher's Cataloging-in-Publication

Burgess, Gloria.
    Journey of the rose : poems/by Gloria Burgess. --
1st ed.
        p. cm.
        ISBN: 1-892864-01-0

    1. Gratitude--Poetry. 2. Faith--Poetry. 3. Integrity
--Poetry. 4. Love poems. I. Title.

PS3552.U715J68 1998   811'.54
                             QB198-1075

Some poems have previously
appeared in print and other media,
including presentations
and performances by the poet.

JAZZ MEDIA
Edmonds, Washington

The author wishes to thank Alfred A. Knopf, Inc. for permission to
reprint an excerpt from Langston Hughes' poem *Dreams*.

Publishing coordination and book production by
Laing Communications Inc., Redmond, Washington
Design and Production: Kelly C. Rush
Editorial Coordination: Laura B. Fisher

Cover Art: The Creative Elf, Julie A. Brockmeyer

Printed in Canada.

For

my daughter, Quinn,
who inspires and challenges me daily,

my husband, John,
who is my rock and healing water,

and my mother and father,
Mildred and Earnest,
who encouraged me to lift my voice
for the sake of integrity,
truth, service, and beauty.

Also by Gloria Burgess

A Yellow Wood

In beauty	may I walk
All day long	may I walk
Through the returning seasons	may I walk
Beautifully will I possess again	
Beautifully birds	
Beautifully joyful birds	
On the trail marked with pollen	may I walk
With grasshoppers about my feet	may I walk
With dew about my feet	may I walk
With beauty	may I walk
With beauty before me	may I walk
With beauty behind me	may I walk
With beauty above me	may I walk
In old age, wandering on a trail	
of beauty; lively,	may I walk
In old age, wandering on a trail	
of beauty, living again,	may I walk
It is finished in beauty	
It is finished in beauty	

Navajo

THE JOURNEY . . .

. . . often begins before we recognize or name it as such.

Mine surely began in Mississippi when I was a young girl.
Ever watchful, often silent, I felt and sensed my way in a
world I didn't fully comprehend. The Mississippi of my
youth was a place where an old world, marked by strife
and racial intolerance, was crumbling and a new world of
equity and understanding was longing to be born.

On my journey, I've encountered "Mississippi," that
threshold, or in-between place, in many guises—in my
relationships, my community, and my work, as well as in
myself. I feel blessed to be able to share through my poetry
some of what I've been privileged to notice and learn along
the way.

My learning has been rich. Most precious is what I've
learned about the human spirit and how imperative it is to
bring our voice, our uniqueness, forward. Then and only
then can we make a difference in the world. I've also
learned that it is essential to daily express gratitude, faith,
love, vision, and integrity.

CONTENTS

Gratitude

Gratitude

a closing of eyes
an opening of hearts
a layin' on of hands

In all things, give thanks.

Common Prayer

Kind words can be short and easy to speak,
but their echoes are truly endless.

Mother Teresa

When you drink water from a stream,
remember the spring from which it came.

Chinese Proverb

When someone shows you a kindness,
express your appreciation, and always, always pass it on.

Mildred and Earnest McEwen Jr.

Wellspring

I have
walked
this earth
cradled
by ancestors.

Four decades
divining
yet only half
believing I'd find
something
whole surging
remarkable there.

Too many years
wandering
abandoning desire
faith intention
dancing with shadows.

Alone.

Parched
in the desert
of my knowing
I crack.

Opened
with remembrance
and yearning
I fall down
to drink in
the font
of my being.

WHISPERS AT DAWN

Hush now.
    Listen.
    Lean into those voices
    that whisper at dawn.

Stand gently
    proudly
    on the broad bones
    the great shoulders

of the grand mothers and fathers
    who dreamt you
        and held you
    keep you
        and walk with you
    stroking your face
        as dawn paints
            that canvas of sky.

THAT AUTUMN MORNING
thinking of Robert Hayden

In memory of my father.
I thank God for his unconquerable soul.

I remember
You leaning
    for balance.

I remember
You before me,
    listing toward earth
    and heaven.

    Leaves dry
    raspy beneath our feet.
    Branches fallen,
    Chrysanthemums faded:
        musty memories,
        dying on mounds
        of autumn earth.

I remember
You steady
    speaking of plots
    as if you were talking about cars or trucks.
    How big (the funeral), what kind, how much.
    Not too fancy. Maple will do.

You lifted
    eased our burden
    even as, moment by moment,
    your body vanished into spirit.

I remember
You in your seasons
    and say a prayer:
    Rain maker. Angel. Guardian.

I remember.

I AM PRONE

I am prone,
borne aloft on the seventh wave.

Above me,
the noble Temple of Poseidon,
dauntless ruins of sun
bleached stone.

Below me,
the anemones,
the white rippled sands
that forever shift
in this dazzling
crystal pool of the Aegean.

From the shore,
blue-green thunder:
the sun-shone sea.

I behold this splendor,
moved
by the ancient rhythms
of this Point,
exquisite Sounion.

ROSE

For the many
who plant and tend
this garden
hands of saffron
cinnamon ebony rose.

For the many
who are drawn
open-mouthed mute
enchanted by the dance
of darkness and light
may they find fragrant solace here.

For the many
who kiss the wind
open their hearts
unleash their spirits
singing tribute

I offer this rose
  witness
     thanksgiving
  council
     prayer.

Faith

Faith

moving with the spirit
seeing with the heart

Faith in God
is the greatest power . . . great, too, is faith in oneself.

Mary McLeod Bethune

The future belongs to those
who believe in the beauty of their dreams.

Eleanor Roosevelt

I knew what I set my mind to do I could do.

Wilma Rudolph

Every young person in America should believe that
with God's help, he or she can make a difference
for good . . . in America and throughout the world.

Reverend Theodore M. Hesburgh

Psalm for Skylar

Before she knew him
    she saw him fly.
No one believed her but
    she felt him grow wings
and with a mother's heart
    she found his name
already written on high.

Driving that day
miles from home
with the eyes of heaven
her mother saw rivers of blood.

    The rest is hard.

    Like mother
    like daughter
    she carries on.

The assurance was all
in the doctor's smile.
Never mind
her body's dead weight.

Three thousand days. Still
she counts, finds solace, gives praise
    she *saw* him fly
into the fold of her Father's hands.

MILAN, 1997

She hasn't worked
in nearly a year
and still
she misses
her boy.

By day sometimes
he visits
sitting by her
all softness and smiles.
Her beloved her
teacher her
tormentor her son.

And in the sobering darkness
more generous
than sure
she utters a prayer:
I don't know who I am
I just know that I am
And I find my way.

Three seasons of grieving
is hardest on the heart.

COMING UP FOR AIR
remembering Adrienne Rich

The ascent
is lovelier
and
longer
than you know.
Having never
ascended
before,
you have no
map, no plan,
no light,
only
pure
purpose,
which is
to survive.

You rise
through
blackness,
seeing
with the faith
of Woman
come into her own,
into

blue green
then green,
then blue,
breaking
the hard surface
into
sun
splashed
air.

Breathing
on your own
again,
why
use words
at all
except
to preserve,
rejoice, and
liberate,
to move beyond
ourselves,
beyond
what we can

merely imagine.

MY DAUGHTER'S SLEEP

Even when I don't see her,
     I know
     she's there.
     Safe in her snuggle
     of quilts and bears.

Emma and Moe and
Snuffles Sr.—the favored den.

Into their downy backs
     she sighs
          and breathes
               and dreams.

SUN

Sometimes
you can wait
for days
or weeks on end. Watching

listening
to fat rain
you might forget
it's even there.
You admire instead
dark fragrant cedars
their shaggy sleeves
cresting and falling
against a steel gray sky.

In thin rain
the mist that whispers
against curling smoke
and crests of quail
you remember
what it's like
to see
the setting
sun
across the sound.

And when
at last you see it
you know
it won't be long
before it vanishes
again
for a day
or if you'll wait
for a week
or more. So you call

loudly to who ever is there
and your heart beats wildly
as those wings—persimmon and gold—
unfold across that expanse of water
a great crane
seeking a new
paradise.

Love

Love

long are the arms
of love—mercy, compassion, service, grace

Love consists in this, that two
solitudes protect and touch and greet each other.

Rainer Maria Rilke

Tell me who you love and I'll tell you who you are.

African-American Proverb

The quality of mercy is not strained. It droppeth as
the gentle rain from heaven. . . . It is twice blest; it
blesseth him that gives and him that takes.

William Shakespeare

Life's most persistent and urgent question is,
what are you doing for others?

Martin Luther King Jr.

Meanwhile, these three remain:
faith, hope, and love; and the greatest of these is love.

1 Corinthians 13:13

Opening

She went to open her heart
but found the key fused
in her hand. Fingering

its cold flat surface she felt
only the furious beating
of her heart. Or perhaps

that strange, wild clamoring
was the first strain of a love
song: *In the cavity of my old wounds*

let new roses grow.

A New Song
for Anya & Nicholas

1. She lay down
　　　on the flat, smooth
　　　　　stones in the river's
　　　　　　　dry bed, stretching

　　her heart in the long,
　　　warm afternoon. Then
　　　　　she heard, for the first time,
　　　　　　　a choir, a burst of sun rays,

　　singing: "Grief is not
　　　precious. Grief is not
　　　　　precious. Grief rises
　　　　　　　up and covers all."

2. Softened by the sun, she lingers,
　　　stretched on the stones,
　　　　　until the moon drapes
　　　　　　　her silky gown, swaddles

　　and cradles her
　　　to her bosom, until
　　　　　the stars lull her to sleep,
　　　　　　　singing his name.

THE DANCERS

What if   and
    the dancer   up
             and
       sprang up

in his handsome
    purple
       body
                did not return
but hung
    in ecstatic
        splendor
                 there
against
      a
        blood-orange
           sky?

Then another
    in an attitude
       of grace
          reaching
            toward the stars

imagine
    her lithe
        silver-threaded
         body

she
    bounds graceful as
            any
              doe
               and grasps
                her lover's hand.

Art Forms

Let the beauty we love be what we do.

–Rumi

A dancer dances
not because he can not write
but because his poems
all torso and thighs
expand and contract
now faster now slower
than he can pen the words
joy longing light loss.

A potter pots
not because she can not sing
but because turn by turn
she composes her music
from water and ash
with palms that trust and see.

A writer writes
not because she can not dance
but because her silky glide her
stomp and funga
compel her
to move
swirl thrust bend sway
in rhythms

and patterns
in quiet retreat
in quiet
retreat
in quiet quiet
quiet
retreat.

Rose in Winter

In the pale blue light
    this December morning,
      he rises only

because he must,
    a pond that vapors
      in the warming air.

He lifts the cover,
    then closing his eyes
      returns to summer

and a rose-peach sky.
    Beside him, she stirs,
      brushing the hairs

in the curve of his back.
    He considers gently
      a moment her hair:

musky coils soft and black.
    She sleeps a long,
      delicious sleep,

shivers, and misses him
    when he's gone.

LOVING

You hold me like a chalice.
Caressing me, all reverence
and grace, your blood flows
with mine, warming, hurrying
my heart. Ten thousand
nights and days
have changed
us.
Bending
towards
each other
again
and for the
first time
we are
drawn into the hearth
of our old new love.

GRANDMA'S BURIED

beneath the mound
of sunken earth
beneath the marbles
in the rusted tin
that welcomes rain
beneath the lilies
that awaken each spring.
toward the back
near the fence
in the old church yard
we found you.
know we are here.

your loved ones
thirty or more
laid you down
and marked your grave
with what they had.
following longing
heeding tales
from northern curbsides
to red southern roads
we found you.
know we are here

restoring the earth
moving the tin
beside the lilies
to make way
for a granite marker
in memory of you
for those who'll come after
who'll tell a new story.
know we are here.
know we are
here who know
You are here.

Vision

Vision

*is not only what we see
it's also how we see*

Hold fast to dreams
For when dreams die
Life is a broken-winged bird
That cannot fly.

Langston Hughes

Imagination is more important than knowledge.

Albert Einstein

The real act of discovery
is not in finding new lands but in seeing with new eyes.

Marcel Proust

If the doors of perception were cleansed, everything
would be seen as it is, infinite.

William Blake

Story Quilt

When I look into your face,
I no longer see a line
of wan blue-eyed burghers.
I delight in
    the Swiss
        Anglo
            even
                German in you.

When you look into my face,
I know you see a line
of proud sable-eyed warriors.
You rejoice in
    the African
        Cherokee
            and
                Celt in me.

And looking into the future,
we see our children's faces,
a boldly patterned quilt,
battened
with courage
and faith
and hope.

CHRISTINA'S WORLD

In that brown
and grassy sea,
everything
depends
on her arm,
bony, pink, and turned
just so.

One hand
tethered
irretrievably
to earth's dark knoll.
The other
a sea bird,
broken-winged,
ever seeking
that marvelous,
miraculous
frenzy of flight.

THE CRANES OF HIROSHIMA

How quickly
my daughter
makes me laugh
or weep.

On the dark stained oak
gold yellow silver white paper
cranes perch in memory
of the dreaming girl
who saw her future
unscathed by the fire
bomb that might
have exploded
were it not for the shrines and all
in Kyoto
Osaka
who knows
these cranes would be destined
for another dreaming
girl or boy

who
    knows.

When she breathes
into the last
she will gather and weave   cranes of love
then let them fly   cranes of hope
gold yellow silver white   cranes of peace
                  cranes of love

cranes of remembrance
cranes for dreaming
girls dreaming boys
cranes to honor
burning dreaming spirits all.

AT ROWAN OAK

In Mississippi once
in woods of ancient oak
I eased into a crystal stream.
Now I see mother and father,

become girl and boy,
wade in waters warmed by some fault
underground. Innocents and magic.
They splash and sing as children do
never minding snakes, broken branches,
impending darkness.

Still, on the nurse log,
pressing down layers of moldering leaves,
what does the turtle see?
Not through wizened openings
in the sides of her head
but with the golden eyes
on her dappled back.

I wonder if she too
foresees my father's crossing.

Integrity

Integrity

to prize the truth; to tell the truth
to shine with the light of your particular star

I am not always bound to win but I am bound to be
true. I am not always bound to succeed but I am
bound to live up to what light I have.

Abraham Lincoln

I will not let prejudice
or any of its attendant humiliations and injustices
bear me down to spiritual defeat.

James Weldon Johnson

Only that which is truly
one's self has the power to heal.

Carl Jung

The more you are like yourself, the less you are like
anyone else. This is what makes you unique.

Walt Disney

KAIROS

I know
    myself
        trailing
            white butterflies
flirting
    darting
        cavorting
            in the cosmos: a mighty sea
                of lavender and rose.

A YELLOW WOOD

Early autumn.
Ascending Mount Si.
Embraced by grace
in a yellow wood.

Generous sun
and a blessing of gentle wind.

Stirred by shimmering,
I lift my face
to the slow golden dance
of aspen leaves.

My heart restored, I am
quickened again
to prayer.

REQUIEM

Forty years
giving myself
away
in pieces

first my music
then my poems
then my laughter
then my voice

Oh
but not
my wings
not my
wings!

Homage

1. Honey   suckle   air
   and watermelon savored to the
   if-you-don't-stop-there-
        you-gonna-make-yo'self-sick line
   collide with pipe drift
   of cherry tobacco
   and red clay dust,
   coloring my Easter egg yesterdays.

   Weepy-eyed hound
   hobbles 'neath rotting chicken legs
   settles in musty Sears & Roebuck paper dolls
   sniffs mudpies sun baked and set under
   to cool just as sure as sweet
   potato goodness on a mother-love crust.

   No place like my honeysuckle home.

2. In the silvered house of God
    men and women shout

> *Hallelujah!*
> *Jesus! Je-sus!*

and nod, wiping
snuffed mouths, crooning

> *Amen Lord.*
> *A-men.*

> *Well?*

3. Dusk songs of field and pond
   give way to love sleep death dawn.

4. Late spring.
    Pilgrimage done.

    Driving slowly north, we
    bid farewell to aunts cousins uncles
    firsts seconds greats and gone. Remember

    Ol' Snake Pond
    where CJ Harper near drowned
    three summers ago
    and his baby sister Jimmy Lou
    did last June
    and the other children's summers
    are not tadpole catching
    or wading ones
    anymore.

Homecoming

Breathe.

You

are

in

your

element.

You are in your element.

Breathe

angel

fish

in

your

watery heaven.

You have found your space.

Breathe.

Song to Myself

It doesn't matter to me
    what you do or where you work.
I want to know
    who you are
    when the sun goes down
    and if you are willing
    to put everything on the line
    to fulfill your soul's desire.

It doesn't matter to me
    how much bread you can afford
    to put on your own table.
I want to know
    if you will knead and wait
    and bake the bread and share
    your blessings at someone else's table.
I want to know
    if you can look into the eyes
    of the young woman
    who sleeps with fear each night
    the one who dared to walk
    away from the hands that pummeled her.
I want to know
    if you can share her pain.

It doesn't matter to me
    what neighborhood you live in
    or what kind of car you drive.
I want to know
    what drives you
    what compels you
    to follow your soul's longing.
I want to know
    what pierces your heart
    awakens you at night and inspires you
    to devote yourself to whomever
    or whatever moves you.
I want to know
    how many times you've opened
    your heart and extended a hand
    to your homeless sister or brother.
I want to know
    if you will sit in the quiet dark hours
    between midnight and dawn listening
    to another's heartsong.

It doesn't matter to me
    how many unspeakable secrets you have.
I want to know
    if you will share your secrets
    to liberate your demons

so they don't devour you
or those you love.
I want to know
 if you will risk looking foolish
 to embrace your bliss.
I want to know
 if you will grasp the sleeve
 of a nameless elder stumbling on his way
 and lead him in from the cold.
I want to know
 if you will throw away your cloak
 and show your heart if you will dare
 to wear your soul on the outside.

It doesn't matter to me
 how many mountains
 you've climbed or will climb.
I want to know
 if you've fallen down
 in the valley of despair.
I want to know
 if you've scarred your knees
 on the stones of self-abandonment.
I want to know
 how long you've been hidden in the shadows
 of hypocrisy prejudice addiction abuse.

I want to know
    if you will stop
    to light a candle and pray with others
    who will surely wander there.

It doesn't matter to me
    what you *say* you will do for others.
I want to know
    if you will act
    with courage and conviction
    if you will daily cradle the frail hand
    of your mother when she no longer
    knows your name.
I want to know
    if you will look into the hazel
    gray or ebony eyes of a stranger
    and say *yes* to affirm your sister
    your brother yourself.
I want to know
    if you will take the time to be still
    call the names and pass the cup
    to honor the ancestors
    who cleared a path
    and broke new ground
    for you and your children.

It doesn't matter to me
    that you have a past.
I want to know
    if you will celebrate your present
    if you will take a stand
    declare yourself sing *I am*
    boldly and with rejoicing
    not only to the stars at night
    but to anyone
    anywhere
    without apologies
    or regrets.

About the Poet

Gloria was born in Mississippi and grew up in Michigan. She now lives in the Pacific Northwest with her husband, John, and daughter, Quinn.

About her poetry, Gloria declares: "I know I'm blessed! Being a *griot*—which in Africa means storyteller—is as natural as talking or walking. Stories are powerful medicine. And poetry is a way of telling stories. Like other kinds of stories, poetry is meant to be read and *heard*."

An award-winning writer and performer, Gloria performs poetry, speaks, and leads workshops for adults and children on finding and expressing their voice. Her workshops focus on creativity, leadership, and change.

If you would like to share your thoughts about this book or kindred topics, Gloria would be delighted to hear from you.

For information about bookings, workshops, and recordings, contact JAZZ MEDIA:

phone: 206 954 0732
fax: 425 776 4640
e-mail: jazzmedia@jazz-inc.com
web: www.jazz-inc.com

JAZZ MEDIA
1102 – 12th Avenue North
Edmonds WA 98020-2512 USA